WRITERS

ON

WRITERS

Published in partnership with

STATE LIBRARY
VICTORIA
What's your story?

THE UNIVERSITY OF
MELBOURNE

WRITERS
GERALDINE
BROOKS
ON
TIM
WINTON
WRITERS

Published by Black Inc.
in association with the University of Melbourne and State Library Victoria.

Black Inc., an imprint of Schwartz Books Pty Ltd
22–24 Northumberland Street, Collingwood VIC 3066, Australia
enquiries@blackincbooks.com
www.blackincbooks.com

State Library Victoria
328 Swanston Street, Melbourne Victoria 3000 Australia
www.slv.vic.gov.au

The University of Melbourne
Parkville, Victoria 3010 Australia
www.unimelb.edu.au

9781760643638 (hardback)
9781743822630 (ebook)

 A catalogue record for this
book is available from the
National Library of Australia

Cover design by Peter Long, Akiko Chan and Tristan Main
Typesetting by Aira Pimping
Photograph of Geraldine Brooks: Randi Baird
Photograph of Tim Winton: Hank Kordas
Les Murray's 'Home Suite' is from *On Bunyah*, Black Inc., 2015.
Reproduced courtesy of the poet's estate.

Printed in China by 1010 Printing.

For Geoffrey Cousins
Thanks for holding a hose

*Home is the first
and final poem*

Les Murray, 'Home Suite'

Home in Australia after too long away, I craved salt water. Jet-lagged, winter-pale, I stroked out beyond the break. Looking past the bobbing line of surfers to the confetti people on the faraway beach, I rose and dipped on the swell. Much later, refreshed, I set out to swim back, feeling fit as a mullet.

Yet the line of surfers remained stubbornly distant, the current a wall of fierce resistance. For more than a year, I'd swum only in sheltered New England coves, where Americans often remarked on what a strong swimmer I was. But I wasn't, not really. And now, as it became hard to lift my arms, I could hear a ragged, rasping noise. It took a minute to realise it was me: whining like a failing engine. I went under, limp with lactic acid, dizzy with hypoxia.

If I could just … make it … to the surfers …
But now that thread of glistening rashies seemed
impossibly far away. I gurgled out a plaintive
cry: 'Mate. I'm drowning.' A blond head turned
languidly. As I gasped and flailed, I heard him
negotiating with the surfer next to him. 'You
take her, Bruce. You're a clubby.'

'Nah. You're closer. You do it.'

I went down again. Then – God bless him!
My bronzed Anzac! – he grabbed my limp form
and draped it over his board. He launched me
onto a wave that carried me to the shallows.
I flopped on the sand, panting.

When my saviour swam in to retrieve his
board, he came up to my shoulder. He was about
twelve. Salt-bleached hair, watery green eyes,
sun-split lip, sarcastic smirk. I would've known
him anywhere.

I'd just been rescued by Loonie.

MEETING THE WRITER I

On a mandevilla-draped verandah, knots of people tangled and unravelled, loud and lubricated. It was the party for the 2004 Byron Bay Writers Festival.

Propped in a shadowy corner, he stood alone, nursing a drink, gazing at the floor. Every now and then I glanced his way. At that point, he'd been a published novelist for twenty-two years, a National Living Treasure for seven. It didn't seem likely he could still be shy. Perhaps the east-coast literary-wanker percentage in this crowd was too high for him: too many people he might describe as 'svelte sophisticate[s] in seven shades of black'. I wasn't game enough to go over and find out.

But when the kaleidoscope of the crowd shifted, I found myself talking to his publisher, and next thing, she was steering me towards him. I can't remember anything about that brief conversation; two introverts making awkward small talk. I do remember that he seemed young to me, which was odd, since he was forty-four and I wasn't yet fifty. The T-shirt and ponytail barely accounted for why I would've mentally placed him in a different generation. Because in the one way that really mattered, he was many years my senior. I'd just finished writing my second novel. He was at work on his tenth, *Breath.* It would win him his fourth Miles Franklin Literary Award.

He'd got cracking on being a novelist, turning down admission to the University of Western Australia and going instead to tech, because they had a creative writing course there and he wanted to learn to *make* literature, not theorise about it. He wrote his first novel and the better part of the next two while he was still a student.

This astonished me. We'd both grown up in neighbourhoods where expectations for achievement were modest, born into families who'd been denied much formal education. We were both beneficiaries of the Whitlam moment, when higher education was put in reach of people who hadn't previously been included. Even so, in my lower-middle-class suburb a girl's desire to be a newspaper reporter was risibly ambitious; the notion of being a novelist was beyond the wildest ambit claim of my imagination. It took more than a decade of journalism and two journalist's books before I allowed myself to even think about it.

Somehow, he had figured it out *in primary school.* While I was doing my long apprenticeship, noting down the odds at a Sydney racetrack for *The Sydney Morning Herald* or reporting quarterly machine tool orders in Cleveland for *The Wall Street Journal*, he was already writing novels.

MEETING THE WRITER II

I n 1991 I was in London, where I was then based, back for a brief respite between reporting assignments in the Middle East. Browsing my local bookstore, I came across *Cloudstreet*. They didn't have a lot of Australian books in the Hampstead Waterstones. An occasional Keneally; a Carey, perhaps. Winton? The name was new to me. I took the book home.

' … one day, one clear, clean, sweet day in a good world in the midst of our living …'

' … the beautiful, the beautiful the river …'

It was an astonishment, this language, biblical in its cadence. Poetic, prayerful. And yet, in the same paragraphs, a mob was chiacking, drinking tea, eating pasties in briny sunshine.

Under a peppermint gum. Not a rowan or a cottonwood from a British or American novel, vague in my mind like the generic green blob in a child's drawing. A twisty-limbed, deeply fissured peppermint gum like the one in Mum's front yard. And here's a Moreton Bay fig – I can see its immense muscularity, feel the cool of its emerald shade – and now a Norfolk pine, and I know exactly how its branches spiral upward, fanning a hot sky.

Then one of the characters says, 'Prolly.'

Three pages into *Cloudstreet* and I could see it, smell it, taste it. Home. I could hear it: our idiom, in all its insouciant vitality, delivered with uncompromising fidelity. Australian writing. Cringe-free. No fucks given if people in New York and London don't get it.

Tim Winton was writing for us.

I looked up from my perch on the couch. Rain

rapped lightly on the window and dripped off
ivy-draped stones in the graveyard across the lane.

'All she needed was summer … She wanted
to be brown and oily on some beach, to feel the
heat slowly building in her skin until she couldn't
bear it and had to run down to the shore and flop
into the gutter between surf banks and have her
flesh fizz and prickle with chill.' Yes, I thought.
That's what I need. To be ten years old, sitting
with my cousin in the back of my uncle's ute,
slapped round on the hot metal, heading for
the beach.

Instead, in Hampstead, evening sucked away
the watery light, draining what little colour London offered in mid-December. It was only three
o'clock. When I went to put the kettle on, my
basement kitchen was stygian. At that hour, in
Sydney, Mum would be taking her cuppa outside.
Around her would be clusters of bougainvillea,

red-gold like the heart of a fire, and ripe grape-fruit as big as your head.

I carried my tea back to the sofa and returned to the ungainly house on Cloud Street, the ungirt lives within. The sounds and smells of that house chimed with memories of the double terrace on Bland Street, Ashfield, where I'd spent my early childhood, trailing after Mum or Dad as they wrangled the odd characters who rented our rooms and paid off our mortgage. Miss Martin and Mrs Patterson, the elderly sisters who lived in dark quarters downstairs; Lutzie, the sketchy conman in the back flat; Goldie, the young newlywed whose kitchenette always smelled of burnt toast. These people spoke in the same cadences as the Lambs and the Pickles, existed in a similar state of precarity and struggle.

I had never read a novel that grazed so closely against my own lived experience. It was an unvarnished vision, meticulous in its recollection of the banal, the mundane and the sometimes cruelly philistine nature of mid-century Australian life; vivid in its evocation of the straitened options of the working class, especially working-class women; subtle but frank in its portrayal of the negation and misapprehension of Aboriginal culture.

But it wasn't *only* that. This was no cringy put-down. These lives were also funny and passionate, full of imagination and yearning, glimmering with the possibility of transcendence. It was a capacious, generous giant of a novel, Russian in its ambitions, Melvillian in its digressions, Marquezian in its flashes of magical realism. All this, but all ours.

Of the Aussie, by the Aussie, for the Aussie.

A FAMILY AND A
HOMETOWN

I arrived at this party late, after everyone else had eaten the good canapés and the wine'd got warm. It was the price I paid for the life I had then, covering news in twenty-two countries, none of them my own. After I left Australia to become a foreign correspondent, cultural fads and movements came and went, and I missed them completely. Dodging shelling in Iraqi Kurdistan and tear gas in the West Bank, or seeing Khomeini into his grave in Tehran, I never managed to order anything garnished with foam or cooked over mesquite. I skipped the entirety of Andrew Peacock's Liberal Party leadership. Winton's ascent had likewise eluded me.

By the time I read *Cloudstreet* in that English winter of 1991, people at home had already started getting over him. 'I think it's time we Easterners stopped thinking of Winton as the boy wonder somebody found on a sandhill; he's already said more than most of us will say in a lifetime,' wrote the Melbourne critic David English in 1987. He was reviewing the story collection *Minimum of Two*. It was Winton's fifth book, counting his works for kids and young adults.

By then, he'd won the Vogel first-novel award for *An Open Swimmer* (1982), the Miles Franklin for *Shallows* (1984). There would be more novels before *Cloudstreet* vaulted him from *succès d'estime* to just plain success, ensuring his books a place not only on school curricula but also in the aisles of Coles. The proclamation of *Cloudstreet* as the Great Australian Novel had been heard in the land.

And, notably, the sound of sharpening scythes had not. This poppy, it seemed, was going to be allowed to grow to the sky. Plainly, I wasn't the only one hungry for the sound of my own voice.

It had been famine rations growing up. My imagination had been thoroughly colonised by the English authors who occupied Australian children's literature in the 1960s and early 1970s. I'd loved Ivan Southall's novels as a kid, but they were heroic infiltrators on a bookshelf garrisoned by authors such as Enid Blyton, C.S. Lewis, Paul Gallico, Charles Dickens, Robert Louis Stevenson and rafts of others less memorable. These English authors wrote about children who wore clothes I couldn't picture (I still don't know what a lisle stocking is) and spoke to each other in an unfamiliar argot. When I finally wrote my first novel, it was about English people. I found it easier to hear their voices than my own.

In high school, the only Australian novel on the level-one English syllabus might as well have been by an Englishman. Despite its bush setting, its fires and floods, Patrick White's *The Tree of Man* didn't feel particularly Australian to me. Even as an unsophisticated seventeen-year-old, I bridled at the snobbery of White's narrative voice. I was repelled by his unconcealed contempt for ordinary Australians, even as he revealed deep incomprehension of the sustaining solidarities, the ardent passions in lives every bit as consequential as those of the patricians among whom he so clearly counted himself.

I preferred a novel I'd picked off the news-agent's rack at the Burwood railway station on my way to school that year. *Thorskald* was a book I'd judged by its cover, which bore a striking impasto detail from an Albert Tucker painting. In that novel, Tony Morphett, better known for his screenwriting, captured something raw and vivid about artsy bohemians at the moment our culture was struggling free of its stifling conformity. Pre-Winton, his descriptions of the beach and bodysurfing were the best I'd ever read.

Casting around for more in that vein, I landed on Frank Moorhouse, and then Helen Garner, and revelled in the familiar, piss-taking wit of the former and the spare, elegant prose of the latter. Both were writing about a recognisably Australian temperament and way of looking at the world. This literature of messy terrace houses and inner-city creatives reflected a kind of Australian life I desired, and one I believed to exist, if not one I had yet experienced. Until my third year at university, I lived at home with Mum and Dad. I crept from lecture to lecture, a shy and watchful loner, confounded by students from more affluent backgrounds who seemed so polished in their self-assurance. It was those students, I figured, that Garner and Moorhouse would want as housemates.

We don't like to talk about class in Australia (Winton has an essay on this aversion, titled 'Using the C-Word'). But while class divides may be subtler than in many cultures, they certainly exist in our own. The political scientist Graham Little deftly captured this in a short essay, 'The Sandclasses' (*Meanjin*, 1971), in which he exposed the class rifts evident even in the supposedly egalitarian ritual of beach-going. I remember reading this, on a high floor of Fisher Library at Sydney Uni, where it had been assigned for a Government seminar. As Little drew his clever contrasts, I felt a thrill of recognition.

In the same way, Winton's fiction is acutely class-aware. And though it remains rooted in the particular conditions of his upbringing, it chimed with my own. As I read his work for the first time, my overwhelming response to it was gratitude. Here, finally, was a writer who had seen us: the unglamorous people of the sunbaked suburbs; the fibro-and-lino folk taking the bus to work on exhaust-choked commutes past miles of used-car yards, but still leading vivid lives against those drab backdrops.

Other responses came later, and with them, a tinge of self-reproach. Here, also, was a writer who had ignored not only the siren song of expatriate cosmopolitanism, but also the gravitational tug of Sydney and Melbourne. He had stayed home and polished his parochialism to a diamond brightness. Yes, Winton *could* write about the rest of the world. *The Riders* is like a tasting menu or an embroidery sampler, showing off his skill at vividly evoking all manner of other places – rural Ireland, Paris, Hydra, the Reeperbahn. But that one novel, *The Riders,* seems to have purged any need he might have felt to engage with places not his own; places, as he writes, where everything that can be done, has been done. The West Australian coastal town is his Austen-esque little bit of ivory on which he works with so fine a brush. 'The truth is,' he wrote in *Island Home: A Landscape Memoir,* 'a family and a hometown will afford you material to last a lifetime.' And for four decades, he has proved it.

In his essays, he often lays bare exactly how his family and his various hometowns have provided the source material for his fictions, down to the grandmother who took to living in a tent in the yard under a mulberry tree, just like Oriel Lamb. The gruesome accidents he describes so vividly in *Dirt Music* and *The Riders* – improvising a tourniquet for a car-crash victim; holding the edges of a child's torn scalp together – are plucked directly from his own experience. The grim Freo high-rise where shattered, downwardly mobile Tom Keely drinks himself to oblivion in *Eyrie* is probably based on one in which Winton went to write, sharing the lift with underpaid nightshift cleaners and shelf-stockers, worn-out people barely making it.

In retrospect, it's a good thing young Tim was disaffected and miserable between the ages of twelve and fourteen, when his family moved to Albany, or he mightn't have such direct access to the alienated minds of his adolescent protagonists in *Breath* and *The Shepherd's Hut*. And while he has survived to grandparenthood in the company of just the one remarkable wife, Denise, whom he has known since he was six, as a self-described 'child bridegroom' he has evidently lived the sleep-deprived miseries of young parents striving to keep squalling infants dry and fed without losing all tenderness for one another. 'Every character is a version of me,' he told Andrew Denton, speaking of his stories in *The Turning*. 'There's a bit of me in every one of them, and especially the really creepy ones.'

Winton works close to the bone. Sometimes, painfully close. And it is this small amount of daylight between his own real life and the lives of his characters that gives them such vividness and plausibility. It may also be why he writes about them in such a particular way. He doesn't condescend to them, nor romanticise them. Winton creates his characters with a full complement of flaws. They are a broken, tattered lot: emotionally stunted, drunken, abusive, reckless, despairing. But he writes them with a careful tenderness, the way a benevolent God is supposed to love his children even when they fail, even when they fall.

AND SPEAKING OF GOD

S omething we, the Australian literary class, rarely do. If religion turns up at all in Australian fiction, it's generally either as the butt of a joke or attached to a character we're being directed to find deplorable. (It's not just us. In 2011, as guest editor for *The Best American Short Stories*, I was struck that in a country where religion has an ever-tightening grip on public and private life, not one of the hundreds of stories I read addressed it, even glancingly.) Since religion has given us both Handel's *Messiah* and abortion-clinic assassins, this aversion is striking.

But Winton goes right there, into what Salman Rushdie termed the religion-shaped hole in modern life. The biblical cadence in *Cloudstreet* is no accident. Winton grew up in a family that read the Scriptures the way my family read the daily newspapers: habitually, fervently, in the conviction that information important to the conduct of one's everyday life was contained there. Fundamentalist, evangelical, it was an approach to religion far outside the Australian mainstream. In all other respects, Winton might have grown up as the epitome of a stereotypical Aussie bloke: white, working class, cisgender. But his family's faith set them apart, alienated even from their closest relatives. Perhaps because of that barrier of difference, Winton landed in a sweet spot for a fiction writer: able to pass unnoticed, safely camouflaged among the mob, but strange enough to benefit from an outsider's instinct, an outlier sensibility.

As he describes in his essay 'Twice on Sunday', his parents' religious metamorphosis occurred when Winton was a small boy, just five years old. His father, John, a motorcycle cop often called to 'prangs' and 'fatals', became himself a victim of a near-lethal crash, knocked off his bike by a drunk driver and hurled through a brick wall. When he finally came out of a coma and was released from hospital, weak and shattered, a stranger appeared, volunteering to help with the heavy work of bathing the gravely injured man through the hard summer of his slow recovery. The stranger, Len Thomas, was an evangelical Christian whose living witness, kindness and compassion shifted the Winton family to an urgent, immersive form of worship.

It's a situation Winton fictionalises power-fully in *That Eye, the Sky*. Ort Flack, Winton's first iteration of the young adolescent narrator, lives in the bush with kindly parents, a troubled older sister and a gran lost to dementia. Not quite hippies but hippie-adjacent, Ort's dad loves trees, keeps chooks, grows veggies, and makes a crust fixing cars for the compulsive gambler who owns the local service station. At the novel's outset, the only dark shadow on Ort's sky-blue trades is the looming prospect of high school in the nearby town, where he fully expects that a countrified dreamer like himself will be brutalised.

But then his father is injured in a truck crash, part-paralysed, brain-damaged. The stranger who unexpectedly shows up to help is an enigmatic evangelist with a murky past, a seizure disorder and unclear motives. Ort is mystically inclined, aware of an immanence that stirs him. Winton masterfully conveys the boy's mix of confusion and enthusiasm as the visiting evangelist tries to overlay conventional gospel preaching on Ort's instinctive holiness and grace.

Reviewing the novel upon its publication in 1986, Helen Garner wrote: 'Winton has kept quiet about his Christianity until now, except in the short story collection *Scission* where glimpses of it flashed unnamed. But in *That Eye, the Sky* he comes right out with it. This novel will kick up a fuss.'

It didn't. Or at least not in the way Garner envisioned. Winton's touch, even when he put his thumb down hard on the scale, was deft enough to provoke no intense reaction. Ort is a baffled, yearning, wounded little boy before he is a radiant soul, and the novel's irreverent, sceptical take on the holy rollers of organised churches makes the book the opposite of preachy.

Few Australians grew up in anything resembling the evangelical intensity of the Winton household, but many of us were inoculated by an attenuated strain of religion. Because my father came from American Calvinist stock, we had not one but two very old family Bibles in our house. Rarely, we'd get them down off a high shelf to look at the page of family names – the births and deaths – carefully inscribed in distinctive hands and different tones of faded ink. But no one ever read them. Catholics didn't do that, and my mum's family – the Irish side – called the shots when it came to religion. My sister and I went to convent schools and dragged ourselves to Sunday mass, along with most of the neighbours on our street of liver-brick Federation cottages. A certain amount of valuable ecclesiastical language seeped in that way – the metaphors in the litany of Mary, the cadence of the Angelus, the archaic grace in certain hymns and prayers. I filed this away in the same mental drawer where I kept treasured poems and shreds of memorised Shakespeare. Like a jar full of beach glass, these glittery shards of finely wrought English were precious to me. *Mystic rose. Star of the sea. As it was in the beginning, is now, and ever shall be. The bread of heaven. To thee do we send up our sighs, mourning and weeping in this valley of tears.*

I just didn't believe a word of it. Despite the best efforts of the Sisters of Charity, I became a godless atheist at a very early age and, contrary to the aphorism, being under fire in a foxhole as a war correspondent didn't change that. I became a Jew when I married, driven by history rather than faith. As Judaism is passed through the mother, I was not about to end my husband's lineage after it had survived exile, pogrom and Shoah. In any case, in synagogues at the climax of the service, they hold up a book and you bow to it, which seems about right to me.

And as the physicist Niels Bohr said about the lucky horseshoe nailed over his door: I hear it works, even if you don't believe in it. I admire the sonorous beauty of the chanted Koran; the glorious excesses of Hindu temples and baroque cathedrals. When you write historical fiction, as I do, faith can't be sidestepped, so powerful is the force of belief in lives of former centuries. All of my novels have clerics in them and one, like the beginning of a joke, has a rabbi, a priest and an imam. For me, it's both pleasurable and challenging to imagine people of faith: austere, confused Hebrews traipsing through the desert, their pain-in-the-arse prophets shouting hard truths no one wants to hear; to make up a sermon for a seventeenth-century minister or to put myself in the mind of a Calvinist girl longing to know if she is damned or saved.

I'm drawn to the struggle. The thousands of

years of human consciousness in frantic search for meaning. All those ancient people ravenous to know how best to live, how to bear the unbearable fact of death. Like Sebastian Flyte in *Brideshead Revisited*, I think the nativity is a lovely story and the gospel messages – turn the other cheek, renounce wealth, care for the least of them – the most rigorous ethical guidebook yet created.

Winton remains steeped in those ethics, though he says he's not the 'God botherer' he once was. 'For me,' he said in a newspaper interview, 'if it's not about love, if it's not about mercy, if it's not about kindness, if it's not about liberation then I'm just not that interested.' In his speech at the 2015 Palm Sunday Walk for Justice for Refugees in Perth, he brought the fire of a revival preacher to bear on our sins. Starting with a gospel text – *If a child asks you for bread, will you give him a stone?* – he raged against 'what is plainly wrong, what is demonstrably immoral' that 'shames us and it poisons the future'. Turn back, he cried, with all the fervour of the prophet. 'Children have asked us for bread and we have given them stones. We filled their pockets with rocks and pushed them back upon the deep. Turn back, my country. While there's still time.'

Love. Mercy. Kindness. Liberation. Ultimately, Winton's books are about those things, poised in fervent tension with their opposites. When I read his novels, the religious concept that comes most readily to mind is the Jewish one of *tikkun olam*, repairing the shattered world. Winton's protagonists are always shattered. Fish Lamb's damaged brain, Sam Pickles' mangled hand, Billie Scully's mauled scalp, Georgie Jutland's alcoholism, Lu Fox's crippling grief, Eva Sanderson's ruined knee, Tom Keely's broken spirit, Jaxie Clackton's abused soul … I could go on. No one is whole. Everyone is in pieces. The question is, always: how many broken bits can be gathered up and made good?

YAHWEH, *NESHIMA* AND *RUACH*

S ince religion is, at bottom, the human mind fending off fear of death, let's stick with death for a minute. There are many ways to die in Winton's fiction – mining accidents, commercial fishing mishaps, lots of car crashes. But one cause of death dominates.

'It's funny, but you never really think much about breathing. Until it's all you ever think about.' That's Bruce Pike, Pikelet, from *Breath*, playing his didj in middle age, finding his way to the circular breath that will animate the instrument just like he, an EMT, has learned to animate a newborn who arrives unexpectedly or to reanimate the nearly dead. As he plays the didj, he reflects on apnoea, hyperventilation, autoerotic asphyxiation, near-drowning – 'the life-threatening high jinks that Loonie and I and Sando and Eva got up to in the years of my adolescence'. These things were, we will learn, much graver than high jinks, and the rest of this finely wrought novel gradually unfolds the extent of the damage done.

If *Cloudstreet* is the embodiment of Les Murray's beloved quality of sprawl, *Breath* is Winton showing he can change the aperture, narrow his focus, and still make something dazzling from a small number of characters acting in a compressed time frame. *Breath* is a contra dance: four people in constant realignment. Pikelet, a cerebral loner on the cusp of adolescence, forms an unlikely but intense alliance with wild, impulsive Loonie. Obsessed with surfing, the two boys come under the influence of the much older Sando, who goads them to ever-greater risk-taking. Sando is married to the moody Eva, whom Pikelet at first finds inscrutable. But late in the novel, when Sando and Loonie have gone off together and abandoned Eva and Pikelet, she seduces and then pressures him into her own hazardous erotic play.

Who by fire and who by water? Who by strangulation and who by lapidation? These deadly fates are listed in the Hebrew atonement prayer *'Unetaneh Tokef'*, on which Leonard Cohen based his famous song. Loonie, Sando and Pikelet often risk death by drowning, while Eva repeatedly risks – and finally loses – her life for an intense, asphyxiation-enhanced orgasm.

In the Scriptures on which Winton was raised, breath is God's first gift. Some rabbis argue that the sacred name of God, depicted by the Hebrew Tetragrammaton YHWH, is in fact the sound of an exhalation. If so, then breath becomes synonymous with God. In the very first verses of the Bible, it is God's breath (*neshima*) that moves as wind (*ruach*) and comes to rest in Adam, conferring upon him a soul (*nefesh*). In the closely parsed teachings of Orthodox Judaism, the words for 'breath', 'life' and 'soul' can almost be translated interchangeably, and the moment of death is defined by the absence of breath, not by heartbeat or brainwave.

Breath carries a similar weight for Winton. No wonder Pikelet bears the damage from those teenaged high jinks into his middle age. In the surf, and in Eva's bed, he has trifled with the very stuff of his soul.

Fish Lamb might have explained it to him. In *Cloudstreet*, Fish is separated from his soul – his full personhood – by absence of breath, by drowning. On the riverbank where he is resuscitated, human will might give him back *neshima* and *ruach*, but not *nefesh*. And it is that severed soul that keeps calling him back to the river.

I think it was John Gardner who advised would-be writers that their job is to continually push a protagonist's head under water throughout a novel, but in the end to decide: are you going to sink them, or let them swim? That metaphor is never more apt than in *Cloudstreet*, which allows both possibilities. Winton lets readers feel the grief and loss of the Lamb and Pickle families as Fish drowns, but we also experience the exhilaration of Fish himself, reaching to reconnect with the immortal part of his consciousness. It is an hallelujah moment, a believer's ending.

More often, Winton's protagonists are swimmers, not sinkers. They are often underwater, but like Pikelet they somehow make it to dry land. Damaged, panting, yet surviving. As in the Christian Gospels, Winton's endings, if not always happy, mostly hold out the promise of salvation.

For people, at least. For nature, he's not so sure.

A WORLD THAT SPARKS
AND FLAMES

L ong before I came across Winton in that Hampstead Waterstones, I had discovered the American essayist Annie Dillard. *Pilgrim at Tinker Creek* fell into my hands in my early twenties, just as I was discovering a passion for the bush. Unlike Winton, whose brand-new Perth suburb abutted pristine – if soon to be bulldozed – bushland, I grew up in the long-settled Victorian and Federation-era streets of Sydney's inner west. A few factories coexisted with the close-pressed houses and I knew the cycles of their manufacturing by smell. A tannery belched the rank odour of death, the Gadsden Hughes can-makers a poisonous fume that stung my eyes. More pleasantly, the aroma of coffee wafted from the Bushells plant on the days they roasted beans. This was not a neighbourhood where one got close to nature. When they tore out the remnant river mangroves at the far end of our road and replaced them with blocks of flats aproned by a concrete seawall, I thought it looked quite nice: I simply didn't know enough to be appalled by the destruction of such rich biodiversity.

I was a reporter for *The Sydney Morning Herald* before I finally spent my first night in the bush. The senior environment reporter was, well, senior – not up to cross-country skiing in the Snowy Mountains back country, climbing the escarpment in Kakadu or rafting the Franklin River. Strictly speaking, I wasn't up to any of it either, but I did it anyway, and it changed me. I fell into unrequited love with the wilderness warriors fighting for our natural heritage, but more profoundly and more permanently in love with nature itself. Annie Dillard became my guide in how to notice and write about what I was seeing.

Early in *Pilgrim at Tinker Creek*, Dillard describes an ecstatic encounter with natural beauty: the school of sharks that 'roiled and heaved' in translucent waves shot with light. 'The sight held awesome wonders: power and beauty, grace tangled in a rapture with violence. We don't know what's going on here. If these tremendous events are random combinations of matter run amok, the yield of millions of monkeys at millions of typewriters, then what is it in us, hammered out of those same typewriters, that they ignite?'

It's such a Wintonesque inquiry. Listen to how it echoes in these lines from his first essay collection, *Land's Edge* (1993). After detailing remarkable encounters with a whale shark at Ningaloo and dolphins at Monkey Mia, he writes: 'I suspect that these extraordinary phenomena and the hundreds of tiny, modest versions no one hears about, are an ocean, an earth, a Creator, something shaking us by the collar, our fear, our vigilance, our respect, our help.' Like Dillard, when Winton walks in the natural world his left foot says 'Glory' and his right foot says 'Amen' with every step. The same thrumming canticle hums through his prose. He notices nature as if it were a divine imperative to do so.

Here's another example from a short essay, 'A Walk at Low Tide', in *The Boy Behind the Curtain* (2016):

... what lies beneath the surface of every sleepy step I take before breakfast: the resonance of a trillion lives, finished or only just begun, subjects that ache to be fed, seek the light and tilt toward increase in a creation that has been burning and lapping and gnawing and withering and rotting and flowering since there was nothing in the cosmos but shivering potential. To tread here and never pay tribute, to glance and just see objects, is to be spiritually impoverished ... Looking deeply, humbly, reverently will sometimes open the viewer to what lingers beneath hue and form and texture – the faint tracks of story that suggest relationships, alliances, consequences, damage ... And ghosting forever behind its mere appearance is its holy purpose, its billion meetings with the life urge in which it has swum or tumbled or blossomed, however long or however briefly.

Winton's use of the word 'and' in this passage has a Shakespearean echo. The great actor Ian McKellen points out that in the opening line of the famous *Macbeth* soliloquy 'Tomorrow and tomorrow and tomorrow', the vital word is 'and'. It is this repetition that evokes the 'petty pace', the weariness of existence to that 'last syllable of recorded time'. Winton's repeated ands, interrupting his busy gerunds, do an equal yet entirely opposite work. They reinforce the plenitude and vigour in a world where not even death is dusty, but vital and life-giving. The single word 'shivering' is also a brilliant choice. It carries intimations of an unthinkable cold in a vacant cosmos where a jelly-like plasma forms and trembles, ready to explode in a burst of light and energy.

But if, as Winton suggests, there is a mandate to help – to steward all of this abundant creation – that's a tall order in a country that has done the exact opposite in its brief post-invasion history. He singles out Western Australians, in particular, as 'great trashers and thrashers ... A state of small people with big bulldozers'. I'm not sure that's fair. If other states had mineral wealth on the same scale as Western Australia, I am entirely sure the level of ruination would be the same. All I have to do is scan today's news to see Tasmania preparing to flatten an old-growth forest for a Chinese miner's toxic waste dump and bulldoze thousand-year-old Huon pines for a scant ten years of tin extraction. Or Queensland draining its aquifer and blowing up the Reef for Adani's coal, or New South Wales despoiling the last remnants of its koala habitat to build shopping malls. We've razed and overgrazed. Asphalted, concreted. Shot and poisoned. Back in 1987, my just-married, new-to-Australia husband, Tony Horwitz, hitched a ride with a logger in the old-growth karri forests south of Perth. What's it like, he asked, to wander in the woods and discover one of the centuries-old, towering forest giants? 'I reckon if she's got two hundred dollars of lumber in her, I'll cut the cunt down.' It was as concise a summation of the Australian extractive mindset as I'd ever heard.

Winton hasn't given up on us, though. He has the cautious hope of a man who, as a teen, saw the beginning of the end of whaling in Albany – the backdrop to his second novel, *Shallows*. When Winton was sixteen years old, the humpback population had dwindled to just 300 and the whaling industry was as entrenched as coalmining is today. But the whaling stopped, and the humpback population has since rebounded to 40,000. The changes didn't happen by accident, he says: 'Brave people made them happen.'

In the early 2000s, Winton stepped out of his carefully woven cocoon of privacy to become one of the brave. He was an essential voice in the fight to save Ningaloo Reef from a massive marina. Since then, he has remained a public advocate, scourging the Perth Festival's reliance on funding from fossil-fuel companies in a blistering speech in 2022. He decried the 'smouldering dumpster fire of business as usual in this country. If we genuinely care about preserving the conditions of life on this planet, we've got to put it out and we must do it now. And I'm afraid that means that all of us might have to hold a hose, mate.'

His wife, a former nurse, has become a marine scientist – steeped, no doubt, in the incontrovertible metrics of measurable collapse. Winton just notices that he has to dive deeper and venture further to catch a feed. That the abalone which was a staple of his family's subsistence in the lean years before *Cloudstreet* has suffered a collapse so drastic that the fishery is now closed. All that bounty, all that plenty, the 'saltwater birthright' of a healthy ocean, now failing under the onslaught of coastal development, plastic waste, oil spills, gas hubs, acidification, overfishing. And most insidious, amorphous and hardest to combat: rising global temperatures.

He wants us to see that there is another way. He writes movingly of the unlikely return of biodiversity to battered properties in the wheatbelt – 'land scraped naked', 'trees exterminated', 'the most sterile and desolate country imaginable' – that have been purchased, destocked and regenerated under the care of the Australian Wildlife Conservancy and similar private philanthropies.

Winton's philosophy echoes the teachings of a nineteenth-century sage, Rabbi Nachman of Bratslav: 'If you believe it is possible to destroy, believe it is possible to repair.' Winton seems to want us to believe that. Perhaps also this: 'God is what you do, not what or who you believe in.' So says Fintan MacGillis, the priest in *The Shepherd's Hut*.

And Winton needs us to get cracking.

BOOKS IN WHICH PEOPLE DO THINGS AND HAVE THINGS HAPPEN TO THEM

'Old-fashioned books', Tim Winton calls them. He has a weakness for them, developed at age six in the library of his uncle's beach shack, where he sheltered from hot winds on summer afternoons. 'I am still that open-mouthed boy, turning the pages, wanting to know what happens next.'

Modern literary critics don't tend to care greatly for what happens next. Plot is unwelcome, even embarrassing: the blowfly in the bisque, the pimple on the wedding day. In his forensic study of the novel, *How Fiction Works*, James Wood, a *New Yorker* literary critic and

Harvard professor, offers insights on character, dialogue, narrative voice, consciousness and language, but has bupkis to say about storytelling. Plot doesn't warrant a chapter; it barely rates a mention. For Wood, it just doesn't matter.

I disagree. I think there's an essential contract between writer and reader: I am going to tell you a story. It will start with x happening, and x will be the most interesting thing I can think of, until y happens. Then $x + y$ will equal an exponentially more interesting thing, and we'll go on together from there.

Winton's novels never disappoint me. They always adhere to this contract. Consider *Dirt Music*. A woman, trapped in a fading relationship, awake and unhappy, sees a cray poacher in the predawn light. Does a runner, car breaks down, gets picked up by the poacher, has sex with him. Woman's bigshot fisherman boy-friend ain't gonna like it. Massive tension, and we're only just getting started. In *Dirt Music*, Winton is deft with character, mood, a sense of place so vivid it vibrates. Yet so much *happens*: car crashes (two), acts of heinous violence (several), a near drowning (natch), even, heaven help us, a plane crash. People do things – rash things, terrible things – and have things happen to them.

It took Winton more than seven years to write *Dirt Music* and on the day he was due to send it to his publisher, he concluded it didn't work. In the frenzied fifty-five days and nights of revision that followed, he says he threw away two-thirds of what he had written. (*Whaaat? I said to myself when I read about this. You mean to say there was* more *plot?*)

Is there such a thing as too much? Not for

this reader. Not when the emotional truth rings through action described in such gorgeous sentences. Helen Garner recalls writing to Tim to brag that she had concocted a 200-word 'syntactically perfect sentence'. She reports that he replied tersely that he 'couldn't care *less* about that sort of shit'.

Why would he have asserted such a thing? It is entirely implausible. He has described himself as working like a tradie, referring to the disciplined way he shows up at his desk just like any bloke shows up at his worksite and toils for as long as necessary to put food on the table. But he also works like a tradie in the sense that he has mastered a craft – all its details, its skills, all its gear and tackle and trim. And that includes sentences of glorious syntactical perfection, like this one: 'Yachts run before an unfelt gust with bagnecked pelicans riding above them, the city their twitching backdrop, all blocks and points of mirror light down to the water's edge.' Or this:

Summer came whirling out of the night and stuck fast. One morning late in November everybody got up at Cloudstreet and saw the white heat washing in through the windows. The wild oats and buffalo grass were brown and crisp. The sky was the colour of kerosene. The air was thin and volatile. Smoke rolled along the tracks as men began the burn-off on the embankment. Birds cut singing down to a few necessary phrases, and beneath them in the streets, the tar began to bubble.

If this isn't perfect craft, I haven't seen it

yet. The gust that is 'unfelt' yet takes visible form in billowing sails. The description of a 'twitching' city – 'all blocks and points of mirror light' – translates what our eyes have seen a million times, reducing complexity to absolute essentials and handing it back to us so that we nod in recognition: yes, that is it, exactly. Same with sky 'the colour of kerosene'; yes, of course, that transparent, faint colour, barely blue, made volatile by heat. This is prose doing the work of poetry.

In an interview with the surfing writer Tim Baker about appreciating natural beauty, Winton comes right out and states his mission: 'As an artist, as someone who writes stories and tries to make words into beautiful forms, it's vitally important to me, especially in a culture that's forgotten the value of beauty.'

So why did he deny it to Helen Garner? What

got into him? I can't say. It's a puzzlement. But perhaps it was a kneejerk rejection of a certain style of academic literary criticism.

LA BELLE DAME SANS MERCI

I n 2013, three years before she left academia to enter parliament, Nicolle Flint took the 'literary left' sharply to task for leaving 'the handiwork of one of our most revered cultural icons unexamined'. In her column for Fairfax Media, she marched through Winton's oeuvre, throwing his female characters off the bus one by one, because each of them had an unsavoury flaw or three.

I thought it an odd argument at the time, especially since it followed hot on the heels of a much-quoted exchange between an interviewer from *Publishers Weekly* and the novelist Claire Messud. The interviewer had opined that she didn't want to 'be friends with' Nora, the narrator of Messud's *The Woman Upstairs*, and asked why the character wasn't more likeable. 'For heaven's sake, what kind of question is that?' Messud exploded. 'Would you want to be friends with Humbert Humbert? Would you want to be friends with Mickey Sabbath? Saleem Sinai? Hamlet? Krapp? Oedipus? Oscar Wao? Antigone? Raskolnikov? Any of the characters in *The Corrections*? Any of the characters in *Infinite Jest*? Any of the characters in anything Pynchon has ever written? Or Martin Amis? Or Orhan Pamuk? Or Alice Munro, for that matter? If you're reading to find friends, you're in deep trouble. We read to find life, in all its possibilities. The relevant question isn't "is this a potential friend for me?" but "is this character alive?"'

It's infantilising and, to me, offensive to argue that novelists may only create idealised female characters. Never mind that Winton's men generally are in much worse shape than the women, each one of them staggering under a dense pack of human flaws and moral failings. But all of them, his men and his women, are vibrantly alive.

I should admit that I am an uneasy reader of academic literary criticism, even when it is not as tendentious as Flint's. So much of it so often seems to take a writer to task for the book they *didn't* write, rather than addressing how successful they were with the one they did. If you want a novel to be about postcolonial settler societies and the ontology of Indigenous displacement, for goodness sake go off and write it; don't write a dense ten-page paper complaining of the many ways that *The Riders* isn't about any of those things. Or, possibly worse, make an even more impenetrable case striving to prove that it is.

Often when I read academic lit-crit, the experience reminds me of reading the annual Amnesty International report. Here they come in their hoods, the professors and the PhD candidates. They've shackled the novel to the wall and now they're going to beat the crap out of it, reduce the paragraphs to a pulp, pluck out an adverb here, a simile there, trepan until the synapses cease firing. And all this so often done in language that is itself a torture – writing that hurts the ear like high-decibel death metal played to break the spirit of detainees at black sites.

I don't want to name any one academic, because there are reams of this kind of thing published in all manner of distinguished journals. But here's just a single example typical of the torture that Winton's novels are often subjected to: 'These tensions are produced by the patriarchal system of signification that structures the dialogue and marks [the character] as both inside the symbolic order yet unable to be contained by it. I would suggest it is precisely these ambiguities, or tensions in the text that provide the basis for a potential reconceptualization of patriarchal dictates of gender and sexuality.' And I would suggest that when I reach for meaning in paragraphs like this one, I find myself grasping thin air.

I think it is more useful, and arguably more just, to ask the question: what is this novel doing, and how well is it doing it? In Winton's work, that is most often an examination of maleness, and most specifically, Australian white working-class maleness, including its peculiarities, deficiencies, blindspots and pathologies. It's particularly ironic that he should be vilified for this at a time when doing the opposite – imagining one's way into the lives and experiences of groups, ethnicities and genders not one's own – is to risk being taken out to the woodshed and thrashed for appropriation.

WORDS, JUST WORDS

Of the technical feats I most admire in Winton's work, it's the way he uses words to convey the inner lives of characters who don't have access to an extensive vocabulary. Many notable writers have fallen at this fence. John Updike, for example: In his novel *S.*, his spiritual seeker Sarah Worth writes letters with the literary skill of, well, a John Updike, and his eighteen-year-old protagonist in *Terrorist* has thoughts of such profound sophistication that he might be a seasoned intellectual in his seventies like, well, John Updike.

Winton has sliced past these sand traps in various artful ways. With Ort Flack in *That Eye, the Sky*, he gets around the difficulty of having a very young, rather unschooled narrator by allowing the child to eavesdrop on extended adult conversations. As we hear what Ort hears, the subtleties of situations are revealed to the reader even as they remain obscure to Ort himself.

In *Breath*, the young Bruce Pike is a more thoughtful, more academically inclined boy but, even so, he could not be expected to bring to bear the complexity of the reflections he shares if he were not recalling the years in question from the distance of his own scarred and world-weary middle age.

It is in *The Shepherd's Hut* (2018) that Winton sets himself the greatest challenge. Jaxie Clackton is a damaged, unloved, misapprehended mess of a child whose sentences are barely grammatical. Somehow, this boy of scant vocabulary must carry a first-person narrative up some of the sheerest cliffs of the soul. To do it, Winton has to suppress his own rich troves of language, deny himself sentences of syntactical perfection but inch his way up those treacherous walls anyway. It's summitting Everest without an oxygen tank. And he makes it work.

Consider Jaxie's tossed-off moment of self-revelation as he explains why he's had to become a fighter, and why he no longer goes to school: 'I wasn't what everyone thought. The thing with the teacher's car come out all wrong. And the business with the crossbow, that never even happened.' Jaxie has form: he is the usual suspect who will be hung out to dry for transgressions whether he actually did them or not. This is why he runs, fearing he will be blamed for his brute of a father's accidental death. Because he always cops the blame. In three concise, economical sentences, Winton has added layers to his character and set the plot plausibly in motion.

Jaxie fears becoming his father and wants to be a better man, a decent man. But with his mother dead and the girl-cousin who might love him living at a vast distance, there's little in his toolbox to work with. Still, as he runs, bluster and profanity give way to glimpses of tenderness. His memories of Lee, his cousin, are all he has to sustain him. 'This is what I got, it's all I got. It's better than anything I ever had before and I'm not saying sorry for it and I'm not backing off, not for anybody.' So, when he runs, he runs towards her.

And on the way he encounters another, differently damaged man, Fintan MacGillis, a disgraced priest living in exile on the edge of a salt lake. We've met iterations of MacGillis before, in *An Open Swimmer* and *The Turning*. In his essays, also, Winton has written about seeking out these loners in their dune shanties, almost stalking them in the search for whatever wisdom such a solitary, exigent life might offer.

But Jaxie isn't drawn to Fintan. He is, by turns, baffled and browned off by the garrulous old man, who is as loquacious as Jaxie is taciturn. When Fintan speaks of coming to terms with his place of exile, this 'rare and beautiful place', Jaxie is nonplussed. 'I think perhaps it's all memory,' Fintan says, pointing to an ancient line of emu and roo tracks in the salt pan. 'Everything that ever happened here is still present now. In the crust, underneath, in the vapours. These days I look out there and it says to me: Here I am, son, still here. I was here before the likes of you and yours were born. Before you even drew breath, I am.'

Jaxie, not knowing what to make of this, defaults to piss-taking. But weeks later, living beside the old man, he is beginning to understand the power of 'getting noticed, being wanted. Getting seen deep and proper, it's shit hot but terrible too.' He can't express this in words, so he sharpens the old man's knives for him as a gesture of thanks.

Until *The Shepherd's Hut*, what I had most responded to in Winton's fiction was his presentation of people familiar to me, whose lives I understood and whose impulses and instincts were recognisable. Lucky me, there was no Captain Wankbag (Jaxie's name for his violent oaf of a father) in my younger life, and very few Jaxies, those few seen only glancingly and while moving quickly away. It's that impulse to retreat that Winton asks me to question: is a bit more tenderness, a bit more attention, a bit less aversion what's required of us if the really shattered people have any hope of gathering up their broken bits?

It is a question that could not be more relevant as we spin away from each other, accelerating under the force of dark matter that we can barely perceive, but that is dragging us nevertheless into ever deeper and more distant silos. Around those high walls, our own opinions echo with a deafening clang, drowning out not only the voices of others, but any voice that even suggests we need to listen.

Winton, steeped in the idea of grace, cries out for our resistance. Chuck a hand back, he suggests. Let's try for less aggro, more agape.

This is the work great writers do. They reveal us to ourselves. They show us who we are, and who we might become. They stand us up where the light is bright – harsh, even – and hold the mirror so close that we can't look away. There's immense consolation in it. When we read, we know that someone else has failed in all the ways we have failed. Someone else has felt exactly as we do. Someone else knows what this is like. We are not alone.

All those years ago, when I fought for my life in the surf of that Sydney beach, I had precise words for what was happening to me, for the fizz and prickle and sparkling bursts of white light. Even as I struggled to get out of liquid and into air, thrashing from deep blue water upward to that azure summer sky, I knew that this was drowning. Tim Winton had told me all about it.

And then he sent Loonie to save me.

BOOKS BY
TIM WINTON

ADULT FICTION

An Open Swimmer (1982)

Shallows (1984)

That Eye, the Sky (1986)

In the Winter Dark (1988)

Cloudstreet (1991)

The Riders (1994)

Dirt Music (2001)

Breath (2008)

Eyrie (2013)

The Shepherd's Hut (2018)

SHORT STORIES

Scission (1985)

Minimum of Two (1987)

The Turning (2004)

JUNIOR FICTION

Jesse (1988)

Lockie Leonard, Human Torpedo (1990)

The Bugalugs Bum Thief (1991)

Lockie Leonard, Scumbuster (1993)

Lockie Leonard, Legend (1997)

Blueback (1997)

The Deep (with Karen Louise, 1998)

PLAYS

Rising Water (2011)

Signs of Life (2012)

Shrine (2013)

NON-FICTION

Land's Edge (with Trish Ainslie and
Roger Garwood, 1993)

Local Colour (with Bill Bachman, 1994)

Down to Earth (with Richard Woldendorp, 1999)

Smalltown (with Martin Mischkulnig, 2009)

Island Home (2015)

The Boy Behind the Curtain (2016)